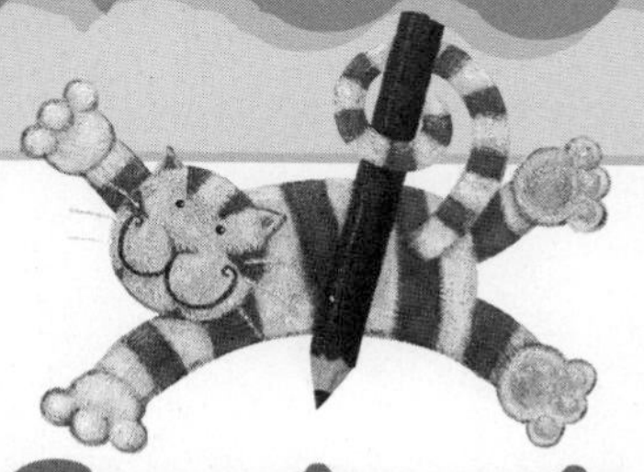

Contents

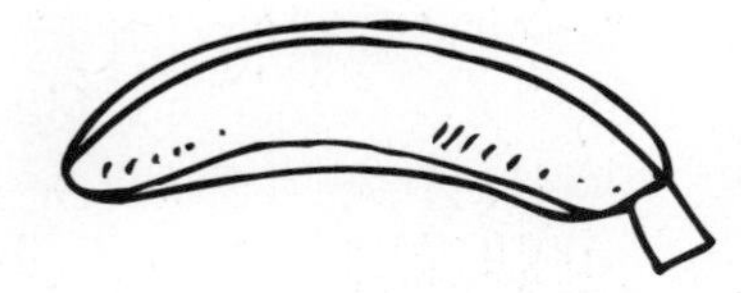

Introduction

Developing sequencing

The perception of a sequence of events or objects is an important early learning skill. Children need to realize that there is a sequence to any activity – a beginning, a middle and an end. Reading, writing and mathematics all demand children to use sequencing skills to make sense of what they are doing. In a different way, physical development and creative development make similar demands when children are asked to think of sequences of movement and sequences of sounds.

There are many ways of developing this understanding and awareness in a young child, but the best way is to involve play and activity so that children can discover for themselves that they can perceive a sequence, follow a sequence and repeat it, if necessary, over and over again.

Once children start to 'cue in' to a sequence, they start to look for other recognizable sequences in the world around them.

The Early Learning Goals

The Early Learning Goals published by QCA are Government expectations for what a child should achieve in education from the age of three to the end of the reception year. Not all children will achieve them, and some children will exceed them, but they are a list of what the average child should be able to do by the time they begin Year 1 of the National Curriculum.

The Early Learning Goals cover the following areas of learning:

- Personal, social and emotional development – developing relationships and good attitudes to learning.
- Communication, language and literacy – listening and speaking in a variety of contexts., using a broad range of words and texts, and lots of books.
- Mathematical development – developing understanding of number, measurement, shape and space.
- Knowledge and understanding of the world – investigating science, technology, ICT, history and geography.
- Physical development – fine and gross motor skills and healthy living.
- Creative development – includes art, design, music, drama, movement, dance and play.

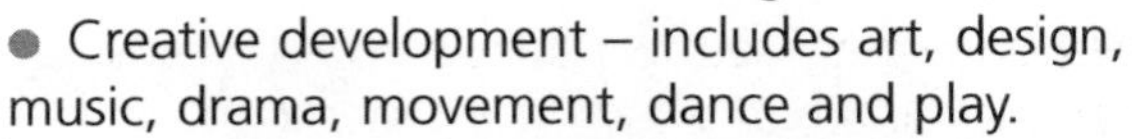

Sequencing is mentioned specifically as part of reading, mathematics, knowledge and understanding of the world and creative development. Throughout this book, the learning objectives have been formulated in the language of the Early Learning Goals to enable the activities to fit easily into your planning.

Baseline Assessment

Baseline Assessment is the compulsory assessment of all children on entry to a reception class. All children have an entitlement to be assessed at this stage in their development. It must be done in the first seven weeks of the term, and there is a requirement for schools to have a meeting with parents to discuss the outcomes of the assessment in that first term.

There are many different accredited schemes nationally for Baseline Assessment, but all contain a common core of skills that apply to all children. All Baseline Assessment schemes must address literacy, mathematics and personal and social skills. Some schemes also address other aspects of the Early Learning Goals.

Because sequencing is an important early skill, several of the activities in this book can be used to identify Baseline skills. These are: 'Polly put the kettle on' on page 4 – Literacy; 'Big Ted, Little Ted' on page 12 – Mathematics; 'First to last' on page 20 – Mathematics; 'Round and round the garden' on page 28 – Literacy and 'The ugly duckling' on page 30 – Literacy.

How to use this book

The book gives ideas for developing the concept of sequencing with young children. Use it as a recipe book, selecting what you want to achieve, what the children in your group need to learn, or what fits in with your long-term and medium-term plans for the year. The activities and their accompanying photocopiable activity sheets are intended to provide short-term planning, but would work best if they were fitted into a much larger topic which lasted for half a term, of which sequencing was just one of the aspects to be covered.

If, for example, you were planning a topic on 'Food', you could include, at various times, the activities 'Bake me a cake' on page 8; 'Oranges and lemons' on page 16; 'What happened?' on page 22, and possibly, 'Polly put the kettle on' on page 4. Alternatively, a topic on 'Minibeasts' could include 'Measuring worms' on page 24 and 'Egg to butterfly' on page 26.

Each activity in this book is accompanied by a photocopiable sheet which can be used by individual children. These 'Individual recording' sheets can be used as part of a display or kept for assessment purposes.

The Skills development chart at the back of the book is designed to help you include the activities in your planning stages. The children can colour in each activity on the snake as they achieve them.

Progression

There is a gradual progression in the book from fairly simple activities to those that require more advanced skills, particularly in the areas of reading and writing. This is to make sure that the book is suitable for, and can be used by, those who work with the older, or more able child, as well as those who work with the very young.

Home links

All of us who work with young children are very aware of the strength of the bond to home, parents and carers at this age. Young children absorb all their opinions and attitudes from their parents and carers as if they were laws, which, to them, they are. If we can harness the strength of this relationship to encourage parents and carers to get involved in their child's development, there should be great benefits to the child. Tact and diplomacy are always essential when dealing with parents and carers, but time spent talking with parents and carers, or spent preparing displays or leaflets to keep parents and carers informed about what their child is learning, is time well spent.

Polly put the kettle on

Learning objectives
To recall a nursery rhyme in its correct sequence, showing an awareness of some features of rhyme; to perform a sequence of actions to match the rhyme.

Group size
Six children.

What you need
Props for acting out the rhyme such as two aprons and a kettle; a toy oven or a surface which can be used to represent an oven; paper; scissors; glue.

Preparation
Make a copy of the photocopiable sheet for each child.

What to do
Teach the children the rhyme 'Polly Put the Kettle On' in *This Little Puffin...* compiled by Elizabeth Matterson (Puffin). Once they are familiar with the rhyme, talk about what it means. Get out the aprons and the kettle and ask two children to perform the actions while the rest of the group sing the song. Do this three times so that all the children in the group can have the chance to be either Polly or Sukey. Now give each child their own copy of the photocopiable sheet showing the four pictures and the words of the nursery rhyme.

Individual recording
Ask each child to cut out the four pictures and put them into the correct order, sequencing the words of the rhyme. When they are happy with the order, let them stick the sections down on a blank sheet of paper.

Support
Use one set of pictures, mounted onto card with younger children. Sing the rhyme in segments and ask each child to point to the picture that matches the lines that you have all sung.

Extension
Cut off the words from beneath the pictures and mix them up. Ask the children to match the words to the pictures. Alternatively, ask them to try writing the words themselves, from memory.

Assessment
Some children may be able to do the spoken aspects of this activity but have difficulty with sequencing the written words. Ensure that you differentiate between these aspects in your records.

Home links
Provide parents and carers with a small booklet containing all the nursery rhymes that you use with the children, and ask them to read it with their child at bedtime or other suitable times of the day.

If possible, illustrate the booklet with the children's own pictures.

Polly put the kettle on

Polly put the kettle on,
We'll all have tea.

Polly put the kettle on,
Polly put the kettle on.

Sukey take it off again,
Sukey take it off again.

Sukey take it off again,
They've all gone away.

Make the bed

Learning objective
To use talk to clarify the sequence of events needed to make a doll's bed.

Group size
Four children.

What you need
A doll; a cot or bed for the doll with a full set of bedding such as a mattress, sheets, pillows, blanket(s) and bedspread or duvet; scissors; glue.

Preparation
Make a copy of the photocopiable sheet for each child. Place the doll, the bed and all the bedding on the floor near to you.

What to do
Gather the children around you and explain that the doll's bed is very untidy and needs to be tidied. Explain to the children that to tidy the bed they will need to know what to do first, what to do next and so on. What do they think is the first thing that needs to go on the bed for the doll to have something comfortable to lie on? Hopefully, someone will say the mattress! Invite the children to place it in the bed. If they do not know the name of something, suggest that they point to it and describe what it is for.

Continue to ask the children what they think is the next item, and discuss what they do with it. When the bed is made, ask the children to recall the whole sequence, and encourage them to take turns in making the bed in that order.

Individual recording
Give each child a copy of the photocopiable sheet and invite them to 'make' the bed by cutting out the pictures and sticking them on the bed in the correct order. The pillow needs to be stuck on first, followed by the doll, and finally the duvet.

Support
Let younger children enjoy using the picture of the bed and the doll and encourage them to make their own pillow and duvet using collage materials.

Extension
Encourage the children to cut around the outlines of the pictures instead of the solid lines. Invite them to make a list of how to make a doll's bed.

Assessment
Observe how well the children take part in the speaking and listening aspects of the activity and assess their ability to use language to sequence events.

Home links
Use the finished pictures of the beds to make cards for the children to take home to their parents and carers.

Provide a short explanation of the learning objectives that this activity has covered, including the physical skills of cutting.

Encourage the children to help make their own beds at home.

Make the bed

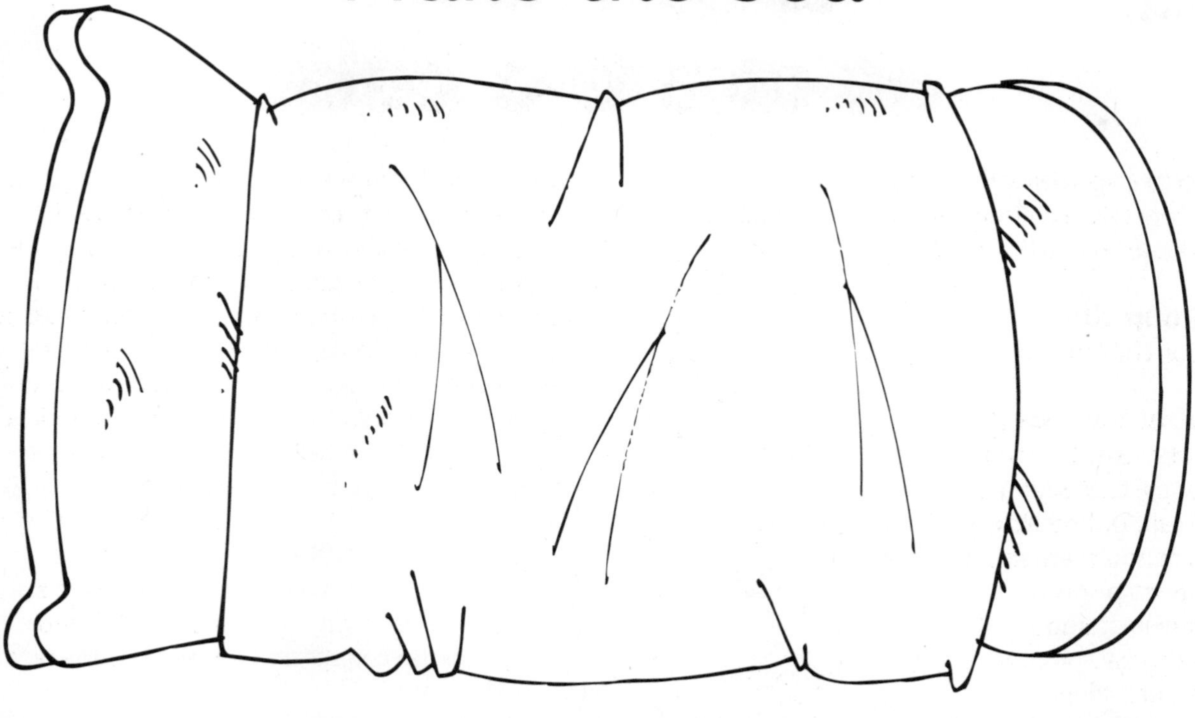

Bake me a cake

Learning objectives
To look closely at the changes involved in baking; to use the senses.

Group size
Four children.

What you need
Ingredients for shortcrust pastry: 250g self-raising flour, 125g butter or margarine, a pinch of salt (optional), water to mix; jam; four teaspoons; a large bowl; four rolling pins and cutters; a fridge; an oven; a baking tray; aprons; kitchen scales; a wooden spoon.

Preparation
Make a copy of the photocopiable sheet for each child. Ensure that the children wash their hands before baking. Preheat the oven to 180°C (350°F, Gas Mark 4). **NB** Check for allergies.

What to do
Let the children feel the flour with their fingers and spend some time talking about it together. Help them to measure out the correct amount of ingredients. Place the flour in a large bowl, cut up the fat into small pieces and then let them take turns rubbing the fat into the flour to make crumbs. Pour in the water and blend the mixture until it has formed a dough.

Leave the pastry in a fridge for half an hour before dividing it up, giving each child a quarter. Roll out the dough and use the cutters. Put the dough circles onto the baking tray and put a spoonful of jam on each circle. Put the tarts into the oven yourself but draw the children's attention to what they look like before they are cooked. Bake for about ten minutes at 180°C (350°F, Gas Mark 4). While the tarts are cooking, draw the children's attention to the smell. When the tarts are cooked, let them cool down before asking the children to compare them to how they looked before they were cooked. Let the children eat the tarts and describe their taste.

Individual recording
Give each child a copy of the photocopiable sheet. Ask the children to cut up and stick the pictures in the correct order to show how they made the tarts.

Support
Provide younger children with a set of the pictures (laminated) from the photocopiable sheet as a useful guide during the baking.

Extension
Ask older children to write instructions of how to make jam tarts.

Assessment
Assess whether each child has looked closely at the changes and used their senses.

Home links
Ask for volunteers to bake with the children. Encourage parents and carers to involve their children in baking at home.

Bake me a cake

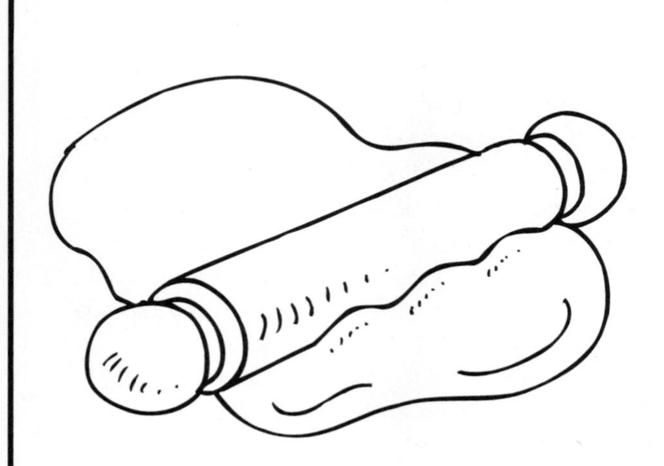

Jewelled bracelets

Learning objective
To recognize and recreate a simple sequence to make a bracelet.

Group size
Six children.

What you need
Coloured card; coloured pencils or felt-tipped pens; scissors; sticky tape.

Preparation
Copy one photocopiable sheet for each child, plus some spares. Cut some geometrical shapes from the coloured card – include a mixture of circles, squares, triangles and diamonds (rhombus). Cut about twelve of each shape. It may be advisable to mount them onto cards and laminate them to make them last.

What to do
Show the shapes to the children and explain that you are all going to use them to make patterns. Start by choosing two shapes and putting them next to each other. Tell the children what they are, then explain to them that you want to make a sequence using these two shapes, so you need to repeat the first shape, and then the second shape. Do this once more and then ask the children if they know what needs to go next. Hopefully, they will copy the sequence until they run out of shapes!

Once the children are confident with the task, ask one of them to choose two different shapes and start a new sequence. If the session is going well and the children understand the concept, you could introduce sequences of three shapes.

Individual recording
Give each child a copy of the photocopiable sheet and discuss how the patterns have been started and need to be finished. Suggest that the children draw the sequence to complete the strips, after which they can cut them out and fix the ends with sticky tape to make bracelets or an armband.

Support
Suggest that younger children focus on colour rather than shape, making sequences of, for example, red and green or yellow and blue.

Extension
Enlarge the photocopiable sheet to A3 size and encourage older children to design headbands using repeating patterns of shapes.

Assessment
By talking to the children, observing what they do and listening to the reasons for their choices, you will be able to decide whether or not they have grasped the concept of a sequential, repeating pattern.

Home links
This activity can also be carried out using shaped beads. Make up some packs consisting of a threading lace and beads for parents and carers to borrow to use with their child at home. Include some cards showing sequences that they could follow.

Jewelled bracelets

Big Ted, Little Ted

Learning objective
To develop understanding of the sequence of size from small to large and the concept of smaller and larger.

Group size
Six children.

What you need
Four teddy bears of different sizes; paper; glue sticks; scissors.

Preparation
Make a copy of the photocopiable sheet for each child.

What to do
Show the children the teddy bears and let them play with them for a few minutes. Encourage the children to look carefully at the teddy bears and to think about what is the same and what is different about each one. Which one is the smallest bear? Put this at one end of the table. Which is the largest bear? Put this at the other end of the table. Put the middle-sized bears in the middle. Which is the larger one? This goes next to the largest teddy bear. Which is the smaller one? This goes next to the smallest teddy bear. Sit them in a row of ascending sizes.

Talk about the bears using the language of comparison – *small, larger, larger, largest* and so on. Ask the children questions about the sequence such as, 'Which is the smallest bear? Which bear is next to the smallest bear?'.

Individual recording
Give each child a copy of the photocopiable sheet and a sheet of blank paper. Talk about the pictures of the bears and ask them to cut out the pictures and stick them onto the paper to make a sequence of bears, starting with the smallest one.

Support
Provide younger children with a set of three bears only – a large one, a middle-sized one and a small one. If necessary, cut out the bears ready for them and ask them to select and stick their sequence.

Extension
Ask older children to make their sequence and then continue it themselves by drawing a smaller bear and a larger bear.

Assessment
Look at the photocopiable sheets that the children have completed. Decide if they were able to do the activity with a minimum of help or if an adult had to give them lots of support. Those who needed extra help will need more work planned on sequencing for size.

Home links
Ask parents and carers if they have any examples of size sequences that they could show to their child such as Russian dolls, suitcase sets or measuring spoons.

Big Ted, Little Ted

Chick, chick, chicken

Learning objectives
To identify some features of the sequence of the life of a chicken; to look closely at some of the changes observed.

Group size
Six children.

What you need
Ideally, the children will be able to watch eggs hatch into chickens which then grow into hens (see 'Preparation' below). If this is not possible, try to arrange for someone to bring in some real chicks. Alternatively, provide some real, infertile eggs and soft toys of a chick and hen, possibly accompanied by a video showing how chicks hatch. Paper; scissors; glue.

Preparation
Try to arrange to take the children on a visit to a farm, where they can see chicks. If this is not possible, read some stories about chickens hatching such as *Hatch Egg, Hatch* by Shen Roddie (Orchard Books). Make a copy of the photocopiable sheet for each child.

What to do
Show the children the eggs. Remind them of the farm visit or the story that they have heard, then ask them what they think is inside the egg. Talk about how the chick got out of the egg and how you would know if an egg was going to hatch. What do chicks look like when they have just hatched?

Look at the differences between a chick and a hen. Are they the same size, colour, shape? What is different about the feet and the head?

Individual recording
Give each child a copy of the photocopiable sheet and look together at the pictures. They do not show the correct sequence. Ask the children to cut out the four pictures and stick them in the correct order onto another piece of paper.

Support
Omit the comparisons between a chick and a hen and concentrate on the egg and the chick for younger children. Let them sequence three pictures instead of four.

Extension
Encourage older children to write a sentence or a paragraph under each picture to retell their own version of a chicken's life.

Assessment
Record each child's ability to identify some of the features of a chicken's life. Note whether they realize that the egg changes into a chicken.

Home links
Encourage each child to take a book home from your book corner that shows the life of a chicken to share with their parents and carers.

Chick, chick, chicken

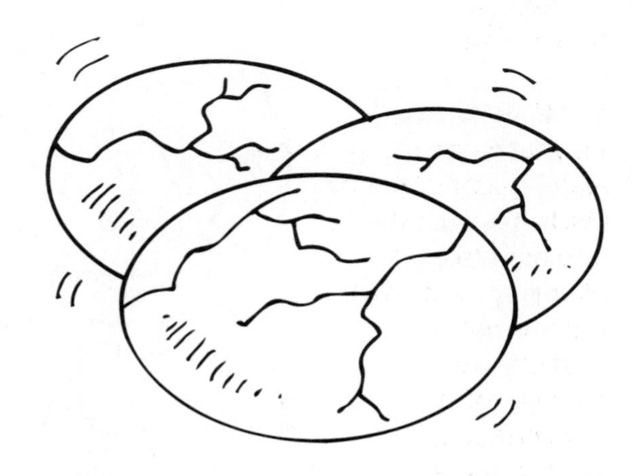

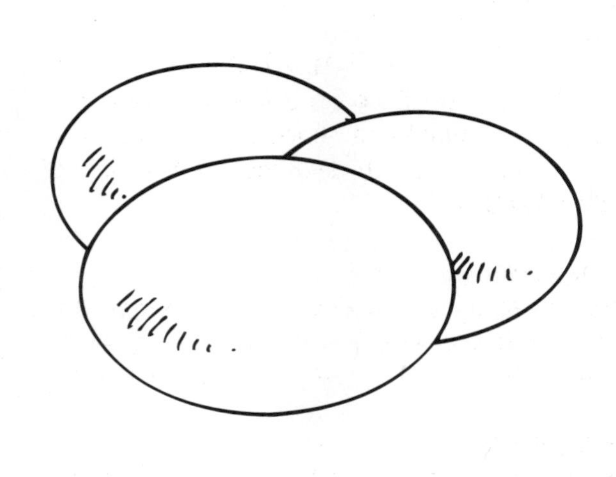

Oranges and lemons

Learning objective
To develop understanding of how to continue a repetitive sequence using actual objects.

Group size
Six children.

What you need
Several different kinds of fruit such as oranges and lemons, apples and bananas; crayons including the colours orange and yellow; the book *Oranges and Lemons* by Karen King (Oxford University Press).

Preparation
Wash the fruit, for hygiene reasons. Select some fruit of each kind which are of a similar size and colour of skin. Make a copy of the photocopiable sheet for each child.

What to do
Talk to the children about the different fruit, what they are called, where they grow and so on. Let them smell and feel the texture of the fruit. If using oranges and lemons, sing the nursery rhyme 'Oranges and Lemons' (see above) while you work.

Make a sequential pattern with the fruit – first an orange, then a lemon, then another orange and another lemon. Ask the children to continue the pattern into a long line. Once the idea of continuing the sequence has been grasped, introduce a new fruit into the sequence and make patterns of three, changing the order for lots of variety.

Individual recording
Give each child a copy of the photocopiable sheet and ask them to write their name on the back. Very young children will just make marks, but these will be distinctive and should be accepted. Talk about the pictures of the fruit. Encourage the children to colour the sequence and continue it using the orange and yellow crayons.

Support
Let younger children make lots of different patterns using two objects at a time such as toy cars, cups, flowers and so on.

Extension
Show older children a sequence, let them dismantle it and then remake and continue it. Ask them to create their own sequence using four objects. Suggest to the children that they write underneath their sequence, to produce a sequence of words to match the pictures.

Assessment
Use the accompanying photocopiable sheet to check if the children have grasped the principle of a sequential pattern repeating over and over. If not, repeat the activity with a different set of objects such as beads, bricks or plastic animals.

Home links
Encourage parents and carers to continue this idea at home with their children using common household objects.

Oranges and lemons

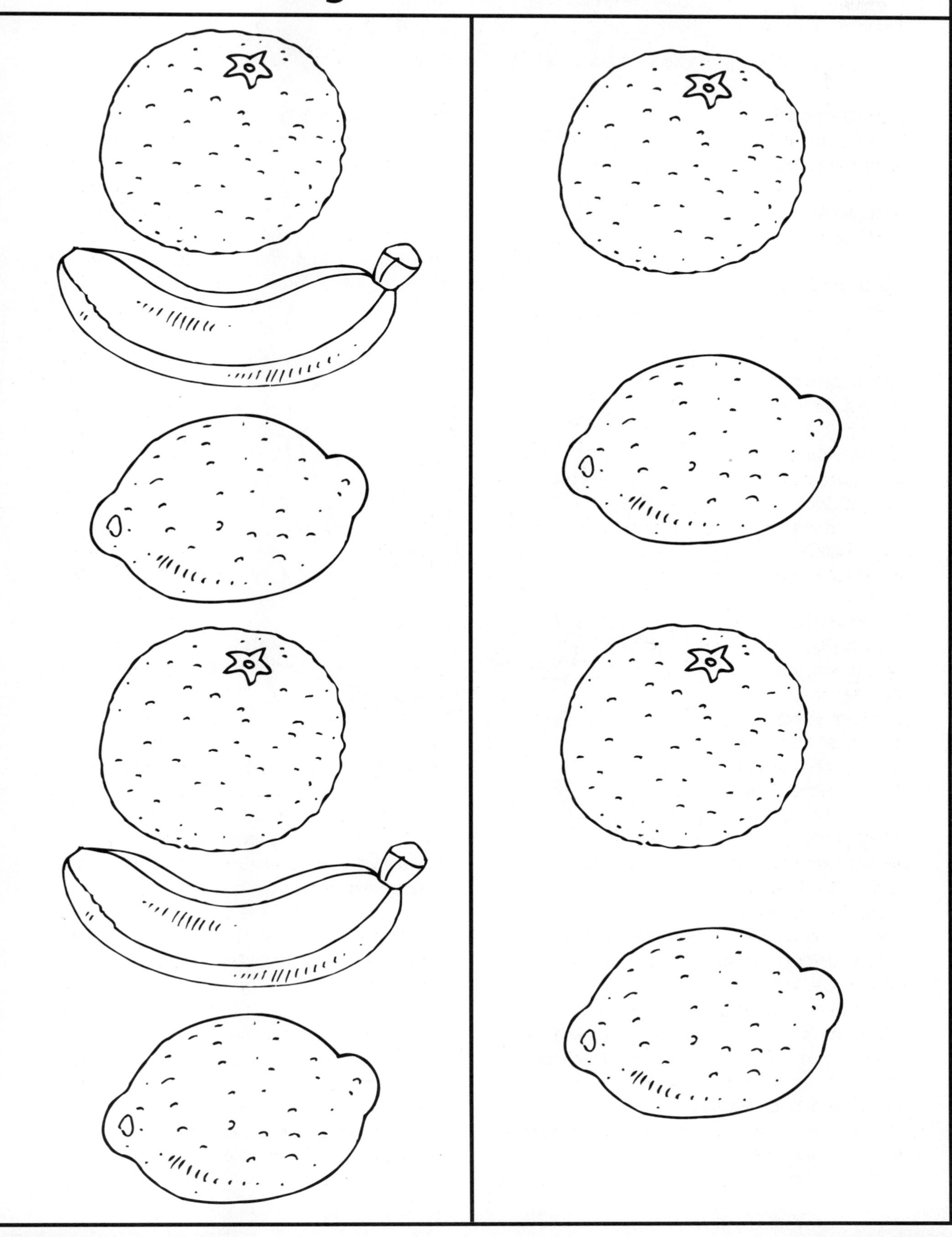

Clap your hands

Learning objective
To explore and recognize sequential patterns in movement.

Group size
Four children.

What you need
Space to move around; paper; scissors; glue.

Preparation
Make a copy of the photocopiable sheet for each child, plus some spares in case some children want to make more than one sequence.

What to do
Restrict the movements you use to four – clapping, stamping, waving and nodding.

Show the children the photocopiable sheet and give each child their own copy, asking them to cut out the four pictures. Now ask each child to choose which of the four actions they want to do first, making it clear that they can choose whichever one they want. As each child chooses their first action, encourage the whole group to join in. Go through all four actions in the child's chosen order. Repeat the process with the other children in the group, encouraging each child to try to make up a different sequence of the actions.

Individual recording
Let each child glue the pictures onto a piece of paper in their chosen order. Encourage the children to take turns holding up their sequence and let the whole group follow it, doing the actions in order, with the child pointing to each picture in turn.

Support
Younger children may find it easier to sing a song such as, 'If You're Happy and You Know It' from *This Little Puffin...* compiled by Elizabeth Matterson (Puffin). Invite individual children to choose one of the pictures and hold it up for the group to see while singing about the appropriate action.

Extension
Suggest that older children start to compose longer sequences of actions, using two or three of each action. Encourage them to think of other movements that they could include, and suggest that they draw their own pictures to illustrate them.

Assessment
This activity encourages children to use pictures as representations of actions and also as a cue. Close observation of the children's actions will enable you to assess and record whether they have understood the activity.

Home links
Put pictures or photographs around the room of the regular activities that the children do for parents and carers to see when they come into your room. This will enable them to visualize what actually happens each day. Let the children take home their 'sequence' cards to show to their parents and carers.

Clap your hands

First to last

Learning objective
To recognize and use the sequence of numerals 1 to 10.

Group size
Two children.

What you need
Felt-tipped pens or coloured pencils; a set of cards with numerals 1 to 10 written on them.

Preparation
Make a copy of the photocopiable sheet for each child. Mix up your number cards so that they are not in the correct order.

What to do
Spread out the number cards on the table and explain to the children that they are all mixed up, and that you would like them to help you to sort them out into the correct order from 1 to 10. Ask one child to find number 1, the other to find number 2 and so on, until they have created the sequence for you. Intervene if you need to, to give a hint about the next number, or to remind the children about the shape of a number. Now count the sequence through together, saying, '1 is followed by..., is followed by...' and so on, inviting the children to fill in the numbers verbally.

Individual recording
Give each child a copy of the photocopiable sheet. Explain that if they draw a line to each of the numbers in the correct order, from 1 to 10, they will make a picture. Let each child choose a felt-tipped pen and remind them that they must start counting with number 1. When they have finished drawing their picture, suggest that they colour it in carefully using felt-tipped pens or coloured pencils.

Support
The first part of this activity, on its own, may be enough for younger children. Alternatively, make a simple five-point dot-to-dot of a house (see the diagram below) for them to complete.

Extension
Extend the activity by asking the children to design their own dot-to-dot picture. Older children may be able to extend their work to include the numbers up to 20.

Assessment
Use the photocopiable sheet as a record of whether or not the child has understood the sequence.

Home links
Encourage parents and carers to provide dot-to-dot books for their children as a useful time-filling activity.

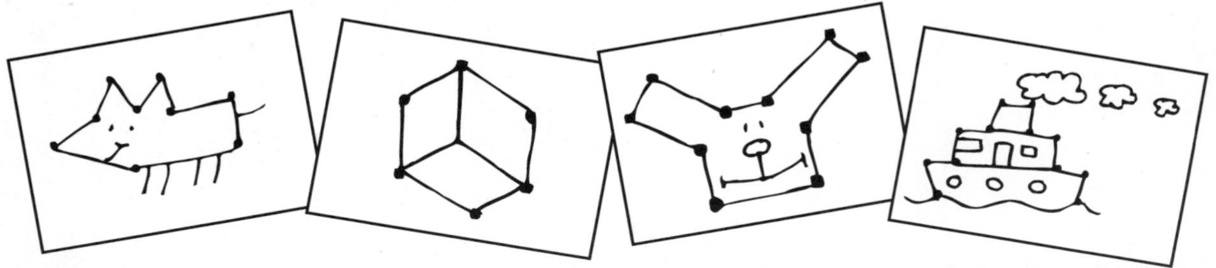

First to last

2 4 6 8

3 5 7

1 10 9

What happened?

Learning objective
To recognize the sequence of an action.

Group size
Four children.

What you need
A plate; an apple; a knife; scissors and glue available (but not on the table); paper; crayons (optional).

Preparation
Make a copy of the photocopiable sheet for each child.

What to do
Show the children the apple. Talk about what it looks like, what colour the skin is and so on. Point out how the apple looks at the beginning of the activity. Explain that you are going to give each child a piece of the apple. Cut it in half and look at what is inside. Draw the children's attention to the fact that this is what the apple looked like after it was cut in half. Cut it into quarters and take the core out. Put the four pieces of apple on the plate and point out to the children that there is a piece each. Encourage them to eat their piece of apple. When they have finished, draw their attention to what is left on the table – just the plate and the knife.

Individual recording
Give each child a copy of the photocopiable sheet and ask them to cut out the pictures and put them in the correct order. Talk about what you started with, what you did next and what you were left with in the end. Encourage the children to go and get what they need to complete the activity.

Support
Select the first and the last pictures in the sequence and ask the children to tell you what they started with, and what they finished with.

Extension
Ask older children to write underneath their sequence, saying what they started with, and what came next.

Assessment
Check whether the children understand what is meant by 'first' and 'last', and that they realize that there is a sequence of events when they eat an apple.

Home links
Ask parents and carers to talk to their children about mealtimes and the changes to the food on their plates at the end of a meal compared to the beginning.

What happened?

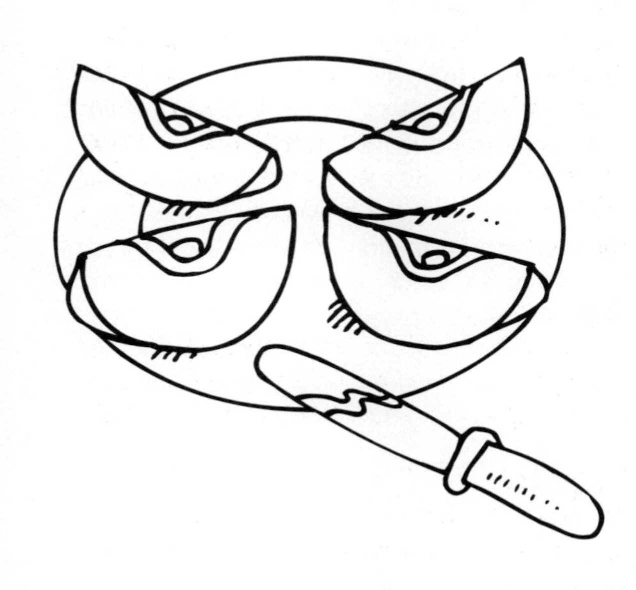

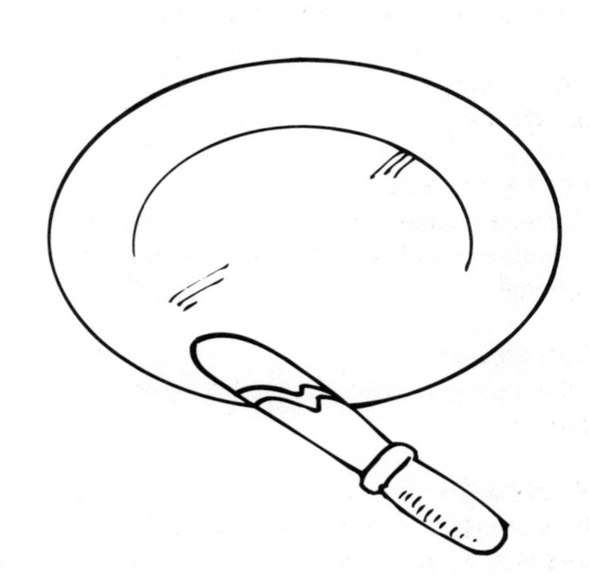

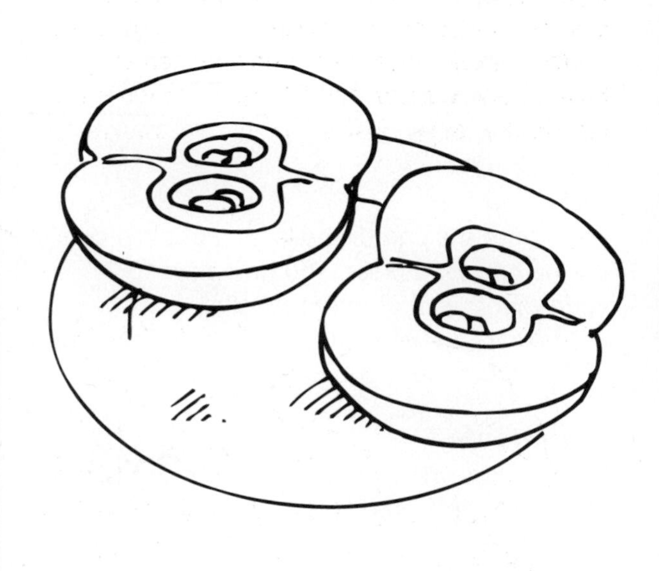

Measuring worms

Learning objective
To talk about, recognize and recreate a simple sequence from short to long.

Group size
Six to eight children.

What you need
Three threading laces or shoelaces (thick ones are best); self-adhesive coloured circles (approximately 2 to 3cm); a felt-tipped pen; paper; scissors; glue.

Preparation
Prepare the threading laces by folding one lace into quarters and cutting off one quarter, keeping both pieces. Fold another lace in half and cut into two, discarding one piece. Keep the other lace intact. You now have four laces of different sizes. Draw faces on four self-adhesive circles and stick them onto the end of the laces. Put plain circles on the back and press. You now have four wiggly worms of different lengths.

Make a copy of the photocopiable sheet for each child in the group.

What to do
Sing 'There's a Worm at the Bottom of My Garden' in *This Little Puffin...* compiled by Elizabeth Matterson (Puffin) or another song about a worm that you know. Tell the children that you have some worms to show them. Bring out your four worms, one at a time, not in size order. Ask a child to find the shortest worm, then ask another to find the longest worm. Put these two worms well away from each other. Hold up the other two worms and ask a child to put the shorter one next to the shortest worm, and the longer one next to the longest worm.

Talk together about how three of the worms are shorter than the longest worm, and three of the worms are longer than the shortest worm. Let each child try putting the worms in order, starting with either the longest or the shortest.

Individual recording
Give each child a copy of the photocopiable sheet and ask them to colour and cut out the four worms and put them into a sequence.

Support
Challenge younger children to use just two worms, the longest and the shortest.

Extension
Encourage older children to draw an even longer and an even shorter worm in their sequence.

Assessment
Use the finished work as a record of the children's understanding of the terms long, longer, longest and so on.

Home links
Set up two tables – a long table and a short table. Ask parents and children to bring things from home that would belong on either table.

Measuring worms

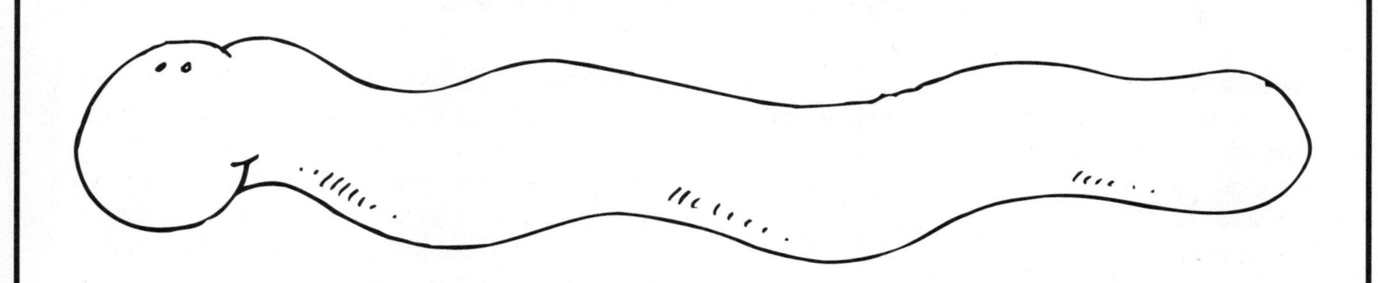

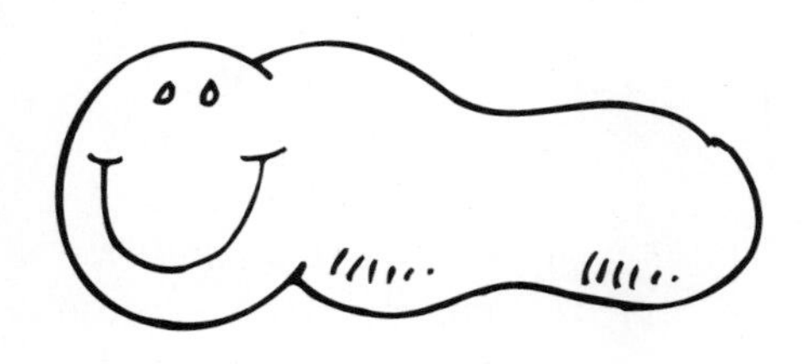

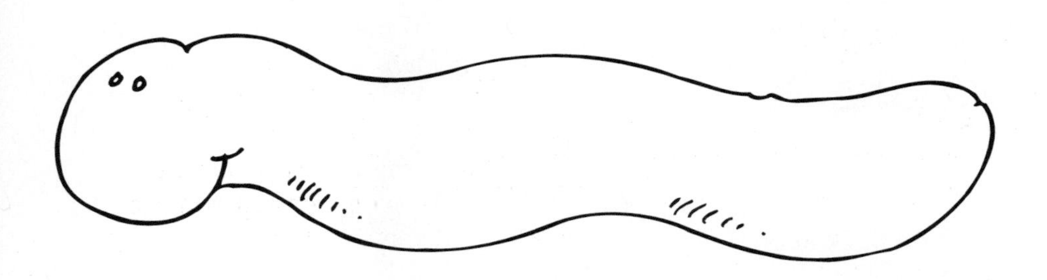

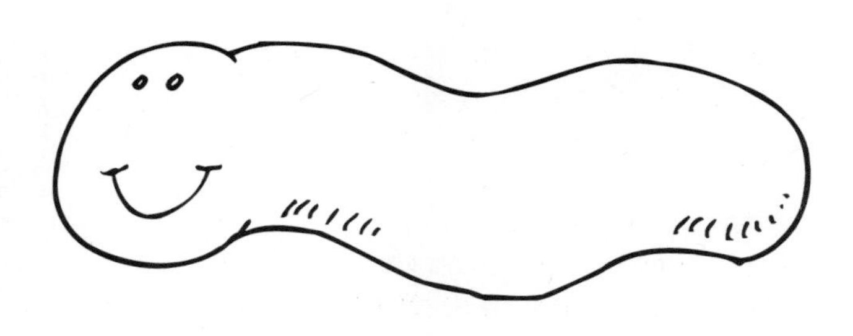

Egg to butterfly

Learning objectives
To find out about and identify some features of the life of a butterfly; to look closely at the changes in a butterfly's life.

Group size
Four children.

What you need
A good, well-illustrated non-fiction book showing the life cycle of a butterfly; paper; scissors; glue.

Preparation
A good preparation for this activity would be to look for eggs, caterpillars, chrysalides and butterflies in a garden area. If you plant cabbage plants, you can usually rely on getting the whole cycle of the cabbage white butterfly very quickly.

Make a copy of the photocopiable sheet for each child.

What to do
Show the children the information book about the butterfly's life. Read it together and talk about the pictures. Point out that a butterfly starts out as an egg, becomes a caterpillar, then a chrysalis, and only after that, becomes a butterfly.

Use the words 'life cycle' and explain to the children what this means.

Individual recording
Give each child a copy of the photocopiable sheet and look at it together. Ask the children to try to put the four pieces of the life cycle in the correct order, by cutting them out and sticking them onto a piece of paper or into a book.

Support
Copy the photocopiable sheet onto card, laminate it and use it as a simple game for younger children. Challenge each child to have a go at putting the pictures in the correct order, encouraging them to talk about the pictures as they do so.

Extension
Help older children to make a life-cycle circle by cutting out the four pictures and sticking them in the correct order on a paper circle. Cut out a square the same size and make a window big enough to see the pictures through. Attach the square to the circle with a split-pin. The children can turn their circle round and round to view the life cycle of the butterfly (see diagram below).

Assessment
Decide whether, in this activity, each child looked closely at the changes in a butterfly's life, and whether they can identify some features of a butterfly's life. The best way to do this is to ask questions and listen to the children's answers.

Home links
Encourage parents and carers to point out butterflies in the summer or to arrange a visit to a butterfly farm if possible.

Egg to butterfly

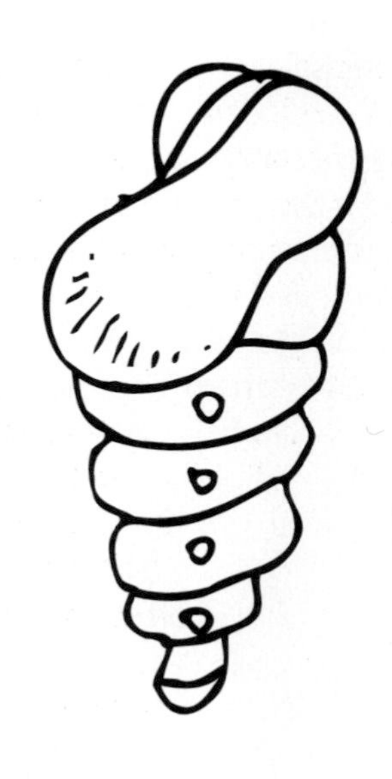

Round and round the garden

Learning objective

To recognize the words in a familiar rhyme and sequence them.

Group size

Four children.

What you need

A teddy bear; paper; glue; scissors; board and marker pen.

Preparation

Make a copy of the photocopiable sheet for each child.

What to do

Say the following rhyme:

Round and round the garden
Like a teddy bear.
One step, two step
Tickle you under there!

Tickle each child in the group at least once, then encourage them to take turns to hold the teddy bear and tickle someone with it.

Write the rhyme on the board, pausing after each word and re-reading what you have written so far. Point out the capital letters and the shapes of the letters and words that you have written. Pay particular attention to the rhyming words 'teddy bear' and 'there', emphasizing them when you read and drawing the children's attention to the fact that these words rhyme.

As you write the rhyme, encourage the children to keep pace with you, continually reinforcing that each word adds something to the verse, and until all the words are there, it will not make sense.

Individual recording

Give each child a copy of the photocopiable sheet. Point out that the words of the rhyme are muddled up and need to be sorted out if they are to make sense. Ask the children to cut out the words and make them into the rhyme by sticking them onto a piece of paper.

Support

Let younger children just use the first line of the sheet and the words 'Round and round the garden'. Say the words for the children and see if they can put them in the correct order.

Extension

Encourage older children to make up different versions of this rhyme as an oral activity, suggesting other locations such as the kitchen, the motorway or the supermarket.

Assessment

By observing and listening to the children you will be able to decide whether or not they have a good grasp of the principles of rhyme.

Home links

Explain to parents and carers that you do lots of rhyme work. Ask them to say nursery rhymes with their children but also to point out words that rhyme when they are encountered in everyday life.

Round and round the garden			
garden	and	Round	the
round	teddy bear	a	Like
step	two	step	One
under	you	there	Tickle

The ugly duckling

Learning objective
To develop understanding of the sequence of events in a well-known story.

Group size
Four children.

What you need
A photocopier with an enlargement facility; the photocopiable sheet; paper; scissors; glue.

Preparation
Arrange to take the children to a local pond or lake to look at and feed some ducks and swans. Make a copy of the photocopiable sheet and a booklet (two pieces of A4 paper stapled together) for each child. Make one enlarged copy (A4 or A3 size if possible) of each of the pictures on the sheet. Make a front and back cover and bind all the pages together to make a big book.

What to do
Talk about your visit to the pond together and show the children the book that you have made. Read the story to the children, then let them tell you what happened on each page.

Go through the book again, emphasizing the sequence of the story – what happens at the beginning and what happens at the end.

Individual recording
Tell the children that they are going to make their own little book similar to the one that they have been reading. Give each child a copy of the photocopiable sheet and a blank booklet and explain that they need to cut out the pictures, which are mixed up on the sheet, and stick them into the book in the correct sequence.

Support
Mount the pictures onto card for younger children, so that they can sequence the story without having to cope with scissors and glue.

Extension
Blank out the writing underneath the pictures and invite older children to write their own version of the story in their booklets.

Assessment
Assess whether the children have grasped the idea of a story happening in a certain order. Observe and record how the children organize themselves to make their books.

Home links
Encourage the children to take their books home, with a note to explain that they have been working on remembering a sequence of events in a story.

The ugly duckling

All through the winter he hid in the bushes.

There were lots of yellow ducklings and one ugly duckling.

Once upon a time some eggs hatched in a duck's nest.

Then he saw some beautiful swans.

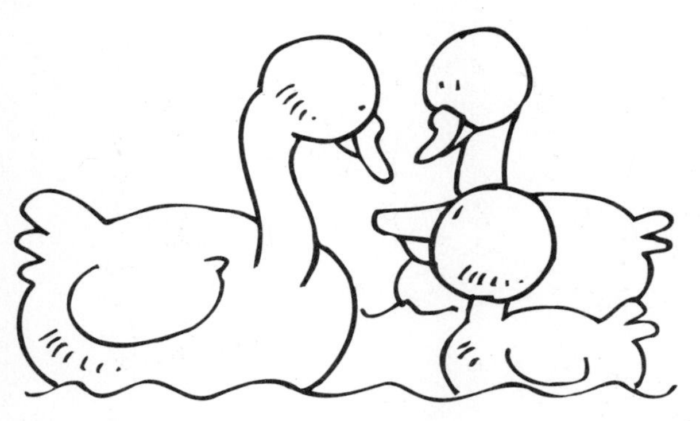

The swans said, 'You're a swan, too'. The ugly duckling was very happy.

The other ducklings would not play with him.

Skills development chart

Name ____________________

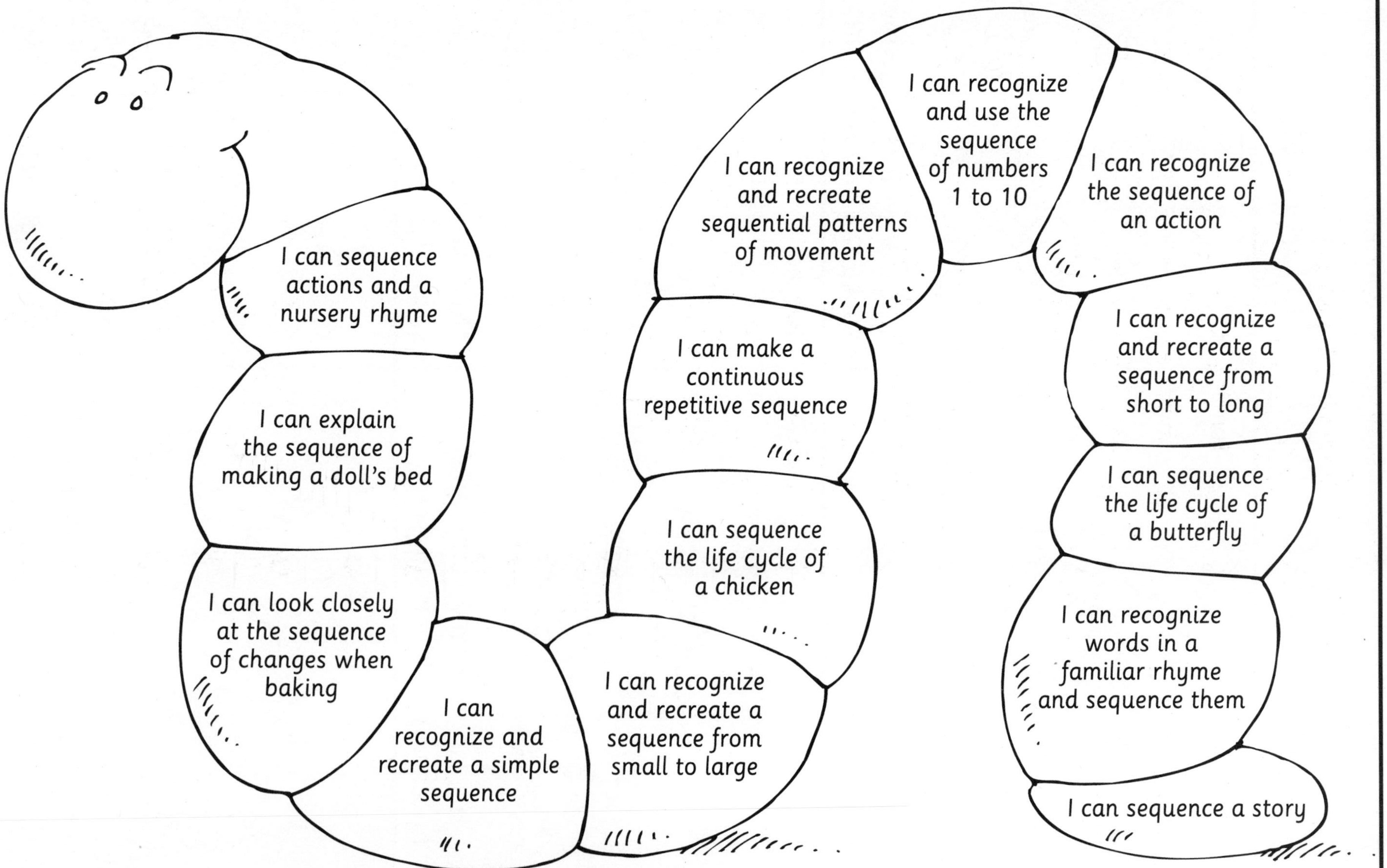

- I can sequence actions and a nursery rhyme
- I can explain the sequence of making a doll's bed
- I can look closely at the sequence of changes when baking
- I can recognize and recreate a simple sequence
- I can recognize and recreate a sequence from small to large
- I can sequence the life cycle of a chicken
- I can make a continuous repetitive sequence
- I can recognize and recreate sequential patterns of movement
- I can recognize and use the sequence of numbers 1 to 10
- I can recognize the sequence of an action
- I can recognize and recreate a sequence from short to long
- I can sequence the life cycle of a butterfly
- I can recognize words in a familiar rhyme and sequence them
- I can sequence a story